For Penny.
Merry Christmas!
Michael
Marianne
Seb
+ Leila

D1223170

Little People, **BIG DREAMS**™

PELÉ

Written by
Maria Isabel Sánchez Vegara

Illustrated by
Camila Rosa

Frances Lincoln
Children's Books

Little Edson Arantes do Nascimento grew up playing soccer on the streets of Baurú, Brazil. Soccer would stick with him forever, just like the nickname he was given by his school friends: Pelé.

He couldn't get a proper ball, so he made one himself out of a sock stuffed with newspapers and tightened with string. It wasn't exactly round, but it was everything Pelé needed to be happy.

One day, he came home and found his father in tears. Brazil's national soccer team had just lost the World Cup final! To comfort him, Pelé made a promise: one day, he would win that championship for his father.

Pelé made it from the streets to the amateur leagues, where he controlled the ball like no other. He performed spectacular tricks with both feet, and scored goals with different parts of his body ... even with his bottom!

A soccer coach convinced his mother to let him quit his job in a shoe factory and move to the city of Santos, where one of the biggest clubs in Brazil was looking for new talent. It was a once in a lifetime opportunity!

When the club managers saw this 15 year-old boy dancing samba with a ball, they couldn't believe their eyes. Still, Pelé would need to keep practicing if he wanted to make the top team. He was ready to work hard.

In his debut match, Pelé scored his first official goal, and soon he was the season's top scorer. But he stayed humble. With his first paycheck in hand, he didn't buy a fancy car ... he bought his parents a new house.

BRASIL

He was only sixteen when he was selected for the national team to play the World Cup in Sweden. Fans all over the world celebrated his goals, as the young striker played his "Jogo Bonito"—a phrase that means "beautiful game."

Brazil won the World Cup for the first time ever and not just his father—but the whole country—cried with joy. Pelé was named soccer's "O Rei," or "The King," and all the best teams in Europe wanted him.

Pelé won two more World Cups for his country and all possible titles for Santos. When he scored his 1000th goal, even the rival players ran to hug him. Bells at churches all over Brazil sounded in his name.

But his work did not stop on the soccer field. He traveled the world, showing how the game could unite people. He also played for the New York Cosmos, under one condition: the club would open training camps for kids in need.

Pelé was a worldwide legend and received all possible honors, from Athlete of the Century to Sir. After 20 years of playing and traveling, he had done more to promote togetherness than any other soccer player.

And little Edson became not just Pelé—the best soccer player who has ever lived—but a person that every girl or boy wants to be. Someone who was just as happy to unite people as he was to score a winning goal.

PELÉ

(Born 1940)

1958

1965

Baby Edson Arantes do Nascimento was born on October 23, 1940,
in the city of Três Corações, 200 miles northwest of Rio de Janeiro.
Nicknamed "Pelé" by his school classmates after he mispronounced the
name of one of his local soccer players, he grew up on the poverty-stricken
streets of Rio's outer suburbs where life was what you made of it. Without
money to buy a soccer ball he had to create one himself—which he did,
from a sock stuffed with newspapers. Pelé's father taught him how to play
soccer, and he saved for his first ball by working in local tea shops. As
a young athlete, Pelé played soccer at indoor stadiums, which increased
his speed and developed his lightning-quick responses. Rising through the
ranks in the youth leagues, he quickly became a future star. When Pelé

1971

2014

became the highest scorer in Brazil's soccer league aged 16, the Brazilian President declared him a national treasure. This was just the beginning of his "beautiful game," which he became known for—expressing joy and happiness as he scored goal after goal on the soccer field. He went on to score over 1,000 goals in his professional soccer career, leading Brazil's national team to many World Cup wins. And his enthusiasm did not stop when he retired in 1977. Appointed a United Nations ambassador for ecology and the environment, he also became a UNESCO goodwill ambassador, dedicating his time to working with children who had grown up in the poverty he experienced as a boy. Today he remains one of the world's most iconic soccer players, who brought joy, dance, and passion to the game.

Want to find out more about **Pelé?**

Have a read of these great books:

Pele: The King of Soccer by Eddy Simon

Who Is Pelé? by James Buckley

Text © 2020 Maria Isabel Sánchez Vegara. Illustrations © 2020 Camila Rosa.
Original idea of the series by Maria Isabel Sánchez Vegara, published by Alba Editorial, S.L.U.
Little People, BIG DREAMS" and "Pequeña & Grande" are trademarks of Alba Editorial S.L.U.
and/or Beautifool Couple S.L.

First published in the US in 2020 by Frances Lincoln Children's Books, an imprint of The Quarto Group.
100 Cummings Center, Suite 265D, Beverly, MA 01915, USA.
T +1 978-282-9590 F +1 078-283-2742 www.Quarto.com
First Published in Spain in 2020 under the title Pequeño & Grande Pelé
by Alba Editorial, S.L.U., Baixada de Sant Miquel, 1, 08002 Barcelona, Spain. www.albaeditorial.es
All rights reserved.

No part of this publication may be reproduced, stored in a retrieval system, or transmitted, in any form,
or by any means, electrical, mechanical, photocopying, recording or otherwise without the prior written
permission of the publisher or a licence permitting restricted copying.

A catalogue record for this book is available from the British Library.
ISBN 978-0-7112-4573-0
eISBN 978-0-7112-4575-4
Set in Futura BT.

Published by Katie Cotton · Designed by Sasha Moxon
Edited by Katy Flint · Production by Caragh McAleenan

Manufactured in Shanghai, China CC052023
5 7 9 8 6

Photographic acknowledgements (pages 28-29, from left to right) 1. Brazil's young international star Pele, portrait, ca. 1958 ©
Popperfoto via Getty Images 2. Pelé's Overhead Kick, 1965 © Popperfoto via Getty Images 3. Pelé, 1971 © Universal/Corbis/VCG
via Getty Images 4. Legendary Brazilian former football player Pele poses with children during the inauguration ceremony of the new
technology football pitch installed at Mineira favela in Rio de Janeiro, Brazil, 2014 © YASUYOSHI CHIBA/AFP via Getty Images

Collect the *Little People,* **BIG DREAMS**™ series:

FRIDA KAHLO	**COCO CHANEL**	**MAYA ANGELOU**	**AMELIA EARHART**	**AGATHA CHRISTIE**	**MARIE CURIE**	**ROSA PARKS**	**AUDREY HEPBURN**

EMMELINE PANKHURST	**ELLA FITZGERALD**	**ADA LOVELACE**	**JANE AUSTEN**	**GEORGIA O'KEEFFE**	**HARRIET TUBMAN**	**ANNE FRANK**	**MOTHER TERESA**

JOSEPHINE BAKER	**L. M. MONTGOMERY**	**JANE GOODALL**	**SIMONE DE BEAUVOIR**	**MUHAMMAD ALI**	**STEPHEN HAWKING**	**MARIA MONTESSORI**	**VIVIENNE WESTWOOD**

MAHATMA GANDHI	**DAVID BOWIE**	**WILMA RUDOLPH**	**DOLLY PARTON**	**BRUCE LEE**	**RUDOLF NUREYEV**	**ZAHA HADID**	**MARY SHELLEY**

MARTIN LUTHER KING JR.	**DAVID ATTENBOROUGH**	**ASTRID LINDGREN**	**EVONNE GOOLAGONG**	**BOB DYLAN**	**ALAN TURING**	**BILLIE JEAN KING**	**GRETA THUNBERG**

JESSE OWENS	**JEAN-MICHEL BASQUIAT**	**ARETHA FRANKLIN**	**CORAZON AQUINO**	**PELÉ**	**ERNEST SHACKLETON**	**STEVE JOBS**	**AYRTON SENNA**

LOUISE BOURGEOIS	**ELTON JOHN**	**JOHN LENNON**	**PRINCE**	**CHARLES DARWIN**	**CAPTAIN TOM MOORE**	**HANS CHRISTIAN ANDERSEN**	**STEVIE WONDER**

MEGAN RAPINOE

MARY ANNING

MALALA YOUSAFZAI

ANDY WARHOL

RUPAUL

MICHELLE OBAMA

MINDY KALING

IRIS APFEL

ROSALIND FRANKLIN

RUTH BADER GINSBURG

MARILYN MONROE

KAMALA HARRIS

ALBERT EINSTEIN

CHARLES DICKENS

YOKO ONO

MICHAEL JORDAN

NELSON MANDELA

PABLO PICASSO

AMANDA GORMAN

GLORIA STEINEM

FLORENCE NIGHTINGALE

HARRY HOUDINI

J.R.R. TOLKIEN

ELVIS PRESLEY

NEIL ARMSTRONG

ALEXANDER VON HUMBOLDT

NIKOLA TESLA

WILMA MANKILLER

MARCUS RASHFORD

LAVERNE COX

MAE JEMISON

DWAYNE JOHNSON

HELEN KELLER

ANNA PAVLOVA

QUEEN ELIZABETH

TERRY FOX

HEDY LAMARR

SHAKIRA

FREDDIE MERCURY

LEWIS HAMILTON

LOUIS PASTEUR

PRINCESS DIANA

DAVID HOCKNEY

VANESSA NAKATE

OLIVE MORRIS

KING CHARLES

Scan the QR code for free activity sheets, teachers' notes and more information about the series at www.littlepeoplebigdreams.com